CALL·OF·THE
WOLF

CALL·OF·THE
WOLF

WILLOW CREEK PRESS

Published by Willow Creek Press
P.O. Box 147, Minocqua, Wisconsin 54548

Editor/Design: Andrea Donner

Library of Congress Cataloging-in-Publication Data

Call of the wolf.
p. cm.
ISBN 1-59543-154-3 (hardcover : alk. paper)
1. Wolves--Miscellanea.
QL737.C22C35 2005
599.773--dc22

2005008124

Printed in the United States of America

"A deep chesty bawl echoes from rimrock to rimrock,
rolls down the mountain, and fades
into the far blackness of the night. It is an outburst
of wild defiant sorrow, and of contempt
for all the adversities of the world.

"Every living thing (and perhaps many a
dead one as well) pays heed to that call.
To the deer it is a reminder of the way
of all flesh, to the pine a forecast of
midnight scuffles and blood upon the snow,
to the coyote a promise of gleanings to come,
to the cowman a threat of red ink at the bank…
Yet behind these obvious and immediate
hopes and fears there lies a deeper meaning,
known only to the mountain itself.
Only the mountain has lived long enough
to listen objectively to the howl of a wolf."

—Aldo Leopold
A Sand County Almanac

Preface by the Photographer

THE FIRST TIME I heard a wolf was many years ago on a cold winter night in the northwoods of Minnesota. The haunting howl of the lone wolf, most likely either signaling his whereabouts to his pack members or searching for them, was mesmerizing. In the years that followed, I've been fortunate enough to have had many encounters with wild wolves in both Alaska and Yellowstone National Park, as well as to have spent considerable time with captive wolves.

I've learned firsthand that wolves are effective predators quite able to take down large prey in order to survive. I'm also a hunter, but I don't begrudge wolves their fair share of the natural bounty in the woods. I've learned that wolves are social animals, and as such enjoy both the benefits and the burdens that reside within the complexities of "the family." I've also learned that wolves have personalities.

Wolves have long captured the imagination of man throughout history. Love them, hate them, or otherwise, there's no denying that this charismatic species stirs the pot, so to speak. It is my hope that these images will serve as both a record and a celebration of this charismatic species.

Denver Bryan
Bozeman, Montana
March 21, 2005

Introduction

THE GRAY WOLF (*Canis lupus*) is one of the most wide ranging land animals in the world, occupying a wide variety of habitats, from arctic tundra to forest, prairie, and arid landscapes.

In the following pages, a question-and-answer format will take you into the world of wolves, explaining where wolves live, what they eat, when they breed, and other facts about these beautiful, rare, and elusive animals. Combined with the stunning photography and audio CD of wolf vocalizations, we hope you enjoy this glimpse into the life of the gray wolf.

Where is the gray wolf found?

AT ONE TIME, gray wolves were the most widespread mammal on earth. Their original range consisted of the majority of the Northern hemisphere—from the Arctic continuing south to a latitude of twenty degrees south, which runs through southern Central Mexico, northern Africa, and southern Asia.

In North America today, the gray wolf is found throughout Alaska and Canada, and in the lower forty-eight states, they have their largest population in Minnesota, Wisconsin, and in Michigan's Upper Peninsula. There are additional, recently

introduced packs in Yellowstone National Park, in northern and central Idaho, and in northern Montana.

There are approximately 2,500 gray wolves in northern Minnesota, over 300 in both Michigan and Wisconsin, and about 8,000 to 10,000 in Alaska. Yellowstone National Park in Wyoming and the Frank Church-River of No Return Wilderness in Idaho have about 270 gray wolves each, and there are less than 100 animals in Montana. The Canadian population is quite healthy, with over 55,000 animals.

"Wolves are not our brothers; they are not our subordinates, either. They are another nation caught up just like us in the complex web of time and life."

—Henry Beston

Is a timber wolf a gray wolf?

YES. THE GRAY WOLF is known by many different common names, including the timber wolf, tundra wolf, arctic wolf, lobo wolf, plains wolf, and buffalo wolf. All of these names refer to the same animal.

There are five gray wolf subspecies living in North America: Arctic wolf (*Canis lupus arctos*); Mexican wolf (*Canis lupus baileyi*); Eastern wolf (*Canis lupus lycaon*); Great Lakes / Western U.S. wolf (*Canis lupus nubilus*); and Alaskan or Canadian wolf (*Canis lupus occidentalis*).

How big is the gray wolf?

THE GRAY WOLF is the largest of all the wild canids, although its size varies noticeably throughout its range. The largest wolves occur in the farthest northern reaches of its distribution. Overall, wolves have very long legs and large heads, with rather small necks for such a big animal. They have narrow shoulders and a narrow rear end, which allows them to accelerate quickly. They also have huge feet, with the paws being about five inches long and four inches wide.

Males are larger than females, weighing between sixty-five and 170 pounds, with an average of

120 pounds. Females can weigh from fifty to 120 pounds, with an average of 100 pounds. Total body length, from tip of the nose to tip of the tail, is from forty to fifty inches in males, and thirty-five to forty-eight inches in females. Tail length ranges between fourteen and twenty-one inches, and their height, measured from base of paws to shoulder, is between twenty-three and thirty-five inches.

Wolves are distinguished from coyotes by being fifty to 100 percent larger and having a broader snout and larger feet.

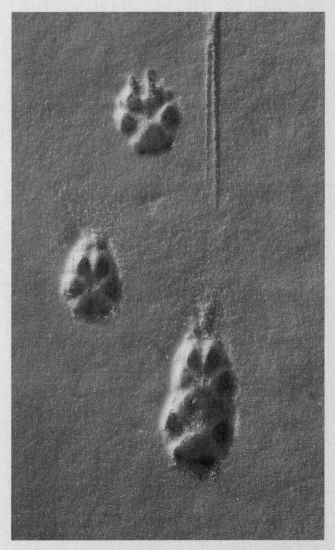

Are gray wolves always gray in color?

No, THEY'RE NOT always gray in color. Their fur color varies geographically, ranging from pure white in arctic populations, to mixtures of white with gray, brown, cinnamon, and black to nearly uniform black in some color phases. Color often changes with age, and most wolves are a combination of colors.

The most common color phase is characterized by varying mixtures of white with shades of black, gray, and cinnamon on the upper parts of the animal. The back is usually darkest, while the underparts are whitish.

How do wolves stay warm?

THE GRAY WOLF does not use any form of shelter except when rearing young. Its fur is extremely warm and consists of two layers: a thick, soft, light-colored undercoat that is similar to wool, and an outercoat of long guard hairs that shed moisture and keep the underfur dry. The coat is particularly thick across the shoulders where the guard hairs may be four or five inches long. By placing its muzzle and unprotected nose between its rear legs and curling its thickly-furred tail over its face, a wolf can sleep comfortably in the open at forty degrees below zero.

"To look into the eyes of a wolf is to see your own soul—hope you like what you see."

—Aldo Leopold

Are wolves related to domestic dogs?

GRAY WOLVES ARE widely recognized to be the ancestor of all domestic dog breeds (*Canis lupus familiaris*). Genetic evidence suggests that gray wolves were domesticated at least twice, and perhaps as many as five times by humans. Artificial selection by humans for particular traits, including size, appearance, aggressiveness, loyalty, and many desirable, specialized skills, has resulted in an astonishing array of domestic dog morphologies.

Why do wolves live in packs?

THE GRAY WOLF is a social animal that lives in packs of two to fifteen animals, although packs of over forty wolves have been witnessed in northern climates. Most packs consist of five to ten individuals, made up of a set of parents (the alpha pair), their offspring, and other non-breeding adults. The pack structure allows the wolves to be successful hunters of game such as bison, elk, and moose that are much larger than themselves.

Wolf packs typically live within a specific territory ranging in size from fifty square miles to more than 1,000 square

"For the strength of the Pack is the Wolf, and the strength of the Wolf is the Pack."

—Rudyard Kipling

miles, depending on the availability of prey and seasonal prey movements.

The social structure within the pack is a strict hierarchy based ultimately on submission to the strongest male. The next dominant individual is the alpha female, who is subordinate only to the alpha male. In the event that the alpha male becomes injured or is otherwise unable to maintain his dominance, the beta male will take his place in the hierarchy. Rank within the pack hierarchy determines which animals mate and which eat first. Rank is demonstrated by postural cues and facial expressions.

Why do wolves live in such big territories?

THE SIZE OF a wolf pack's territory is determined by the number of prey species living within that area and the number of wolves competing for the same prey. Territories may overlap slightly, but packs usually avoid one another. If food is adequate, a pack may use the same home range for several generations.

Wolves travel their territory every day, but the length of the journey changes depending on the time of year. In the fall and winter, when the pack is not maintaining a den site, the animals wander further and do not necessarily return to a particular

"We listened for a voice crying in the wilderness. And we heard the jubilation of wolves!"

—Durwood L. Allen

location each day. Wolf movements are usually at night and over long distances.

Wolves tend to move in single file, generally visiting lakes, rivers, and streams where prey accumulate. Wolves often travel in excess of twenty miles in one day, covering the territory in a characteristic trot of four to five miles an hour. Although wolves can attain speeds as high as forty-five miles per hour for short distances, most hunting pursuits are designed to identify weak prey species, and a prolonged chase of eight to ten miles per hour is normal.

"One is more likely to come upon the tracks of a wolf than to come upon the wolf who made them."

—Unknown

What do wolves eat?

THE GRAY WOLF is primarily a
predator of mammals larger than
itself, such as deer, elk, moose,
bison, and mountain sheep. They
generally hunt in packs consist-
ing of all the adults and yearlings
that are not guarding the pups, as
it takes several wolves to
efficiently and safely bring down
the larger prey.

Each hunt varies on circum-
stance, prey type, and pack com-
position and size, but in general,
they simply outrun the prey
species, drag it down, and tear at
it until it is too weak to fend off
the pack. Prey is located by
chance encounter, airborne scent,

or following a fresh scent trail on the ground or in the snow.

Wolves tend to kill the young, old, and sick, which are often nutritionally stressed or physically burdened. Wolf kill rates are the highest in the winter months when wolves gain an advantage over large prey in the snow. The pack generally stalks prey, when conditions allow, to get as close as possible and save energy. The stalk also allows the wolves to evaluate the overall condition of the prey species and identify any individuals showing signs of weakness or distress.

Once a kill has been made by the pack, wolves generally consume large amounts of meat

"The caribou feeds the wolf, but it is the wolf who keeps the caribou strong."

—Keewation (Inuit) proverb

in a noisy, snarling scramble most often dominated by the alpha male and female.

An adult wolf needs about four pounds of food per day, but requires about five pounds per day to successfully reproduce. Wolves can go for two weeks or more without food. On average, wolves eat ten pounds of food per day, but because of their feast or famine lifestyle, wolves will gorge on more the twenty pounds of meat when a kill is made. The pack will remain in the vicinity of a kill for several days until the remains have been consumed.

When do wolves breed?

"Wolf is the Grand Teacher. Wolf is the sage, who after many winters upon the sacred path and seeking the ways of wisdom, returns to share new knowledge with the tribe. Wolf is both the radical and the traditional in the same breath."

—Robert Ghost Wolf

THE LIFE OF THE pack keeps an annual rhythm. In deep winter, when the dominant female comes into estrus, social tension increases in the pack. As the dominant female becomes fertile, both she and the alpha male become increasingly aggressive toward subordinates.

Within the pack structure, only the alpha pair is likely to breed. Their aggressive behavior deters other members of the pack from mating, ensuring the best chance of survival for the leader's pups. Once mating has occurred, tension in the pack subsides.

Breeding occurs between the

months of January and April, with northern populations breeding later in the season than southern populations. Female gray wolves come into estrus once each year and mating occurs during this time.

Female gray wolves choose their mates and often form a lifelong pair bond. This pair is monogamous, although a new alpha male or female will emerge with the death of an alpha individual. Gray wolf pairs spend a great deal of time together.

Where are the pups born?

AFTER MATING occurs, the female digs a den in which to raise her young. Dens are often used year after year, but wolves may also dig new dens or use some type of shelter, such as a cave or the area beneath a cliff or fallen tree.

The dens are used only for rearing young, and are often situated in elevated areas near water. They also often feature tunnels extending up to twenty feet from the entrance that lead to an enlarged underground chamber. There are often a number of entrances to the den, each marked with a pile of excavated soil.

How many pups are usually born?

AFTER A gestation period of sixty to sixty-three days, the pups are born. Litter size ranges from one to fifteen pups, but on average six to seven pups are born. The pups remain in the den until they are eight to ten weeks old. Females stay with their pups almost exclusively for the first three weeks,. The pups are completely dependent on their mother for the first two months of life until they are weaned.

When do the pups leave the den?

BORN BLIND AND deaf, the pups typically open their eyes during their second week, and they begin to explore outside the den by three weeks when they are able to stand, walk, and vocalize.

The pups will remain near the den until they are several months old. They play fight with each other and are fed regurgitated, partially digested meals from all members of the pack. As the pups age, pack members will stop regurgitating meals and bring back meat from their hunting successes for them to eat.

At about two months of age, the adults move the pups to a

meadow or similar open area that is known as a "rendezvous site." The pack will often assemble around the rendezvous site and leave the young there, sometimes with a subordinate adult babysitter and sometimes without one, while the adults go off to hunt. A pack may change rendezvous sites several times during the summer as they follow prey or are disturbed by humans.

Wolf pups develop rapidly; they must be large and accomplished enough to hunt with the pack with the onset of winter. When the pups are seven to eight months old and almost fully grown, they begin traveling with the adults.

"Wolves may feature in our myths, our history, and our dreams, but they have their own future, their own loves, their own dreams to fulfill."

—Anthony Miles

Interactions during the pups first months of life, as well as the dominance status of the mother, ultimately determine their position in the strong pack hierarchy. Usually, between one and three years of age, a young wolf leaves and tries to find a mate and form its own pack. During this time, lone wolves typically eat much smaller mammals that they can hunt and take down on their own. Lone dispersing wolves have traveled as far as 500 miles in search of a new home.

How is the pack hierarchy maintained?

THE ALPHA MALE, who is dominant over all other individuals, and the alpha female, who is subordinate only to the alpha male, communicate their dominance through body language, aggression, and facial expressions. A dominant wolf may only need to stare at a subordinate to freeze it in its tracks.

Subordinate wolves will crouch, lower their heads, and roll over on their backs to show deference to the alpha pair. When the pack reassembles after a hunt, they take part in elaborate displays of greeting in which all members gather

"Wolves are fiercely loyal to their mates, have a strong sense of family, yet maintain their individualism... qualities we admire in ourselves."

—Unknown

around the dominant male with their ears back and eyes narrowed in submission and pleasure. They will also nuzzle his face and lick his jaws. An inferior wolf will also tuck its tail under its body, and not look any dominant wolf in the eyes for a long period of time.

Social status within the pack is rather consistent, and the alpha male and female may retain their positions for years. The alpha male will be challenged by subordinate males or outsiders if he becomes vulnerable through injury or old age.

Why do wolves howl?

WOLVES ARE NOTED for their distinctive howl, which they use as a form of communication. The main reason wolves howl is to locate each other after they've been separated. Because they range over vast areas to find food, wolves are often separated from one another. Howling enables them to call to each other over great distances. The low pitch and long duration of a howl are well suited for transmission in the forest and across the tundra.

Another reason wolves howl is to defend their territory from rival packs. When one pack howls, others nearby may reply,

"Anyone who has ever heard it when the land was covered with a blanket of snow and elusively lighted by shimmering moonlight, will never forget the strange, trembling wolf cry."

—Unknown

and very quickly, all the wolves know each other's location. By advertising their presence, packs can communicate the boundaries of their territories and avoid accidentally running into each other. Wolves also howl to pass on an alarm, especially at the den site.

Wolves howl more frequently in the evening and early morning, and during winter-breeding and pup rearing. When wolves howl together, each wolf chooses a different pitch, which creates the impression of fifteen or twenty wolves when there are actually only three or four.

"How lonely is the night without the howl of a wolf."

—Unknown

Do wolves bark, like dogs do?

THE OTHER vocalizations made by wolves are barks, yips, squeaks and whines. Wolves do not bark often, however, and when they do, it is a quiet "woof" more often than a dog-like bark. They also do not bark continuously like dogs but "woof" a few times and then stop. Wolves typically bark when they are surprised and use it as a warning to the other members of the pack.

Wolves growl over food challenges and when they are threatened. They whine and squeak in greeting, during play, when feeding the pups, and during other friendly social activities.

Do pups instinctively howl?

YES, WOLF PUPS instinctively howl as early as four weeks old. The pups will indiscriminately howl or respond to an adult howling near the den site. It is usually safe for them to howl near the den or the rendezvous site because these areas are relatively far from other packs. Replying to a howling adult also often leads to a meal, since wolves returning with food frequently howl as they near the home site. Once pups start to travel with the pack, however, they begin to enter less secure surroundings, and by six months of age, they are as selective as adult wolves about where and when they howl.

In what other ways do wolves communicate?

A<small>S</small> SOCIAL ANIMALS living in family groups, wolves are constantly interacting with each other, and one notable social behavior is how often they display a spirit of friendliness and cooperation. Whenever the pack gets up from a rest or leaves a kill, there is likely to be a play session. They often play games of keep-away with bits of stick or bone, and they often pounce on each other and wrestle in mock battle. Both pups and adults play at hunting behavior, stalking, ambushing, and chasing. This kind of friendly play helps maintain the close coordination wolves need for hunting.

"The wolf's clear, intelligent eyes brushed mine. The wolf is gentle-hearted. Not noble, not cowardly, just non-fighting."

—Lois Crisler

Why have the gray wolf's population and distribution changed so dramatically?

THE GRAY WOLF became nearly extinct in the lower forty-eight states in the early part of the twentieth century because settlers believed wolves caused widespread livestock losses.

Early settlers moving westward severely depleted most populations of bison, deer, elk, and moose—animals that were important prey for wolves. With little alternative, wolves turned to sheep and cattle that had replaced their natural prey. To protect livestock, ranchers and government agencies began a

campaign to eliminate wolves. Bounty programs initiated in the nineteenth century continued as late as 1965, offering twenty to fifty dollars per wolf. Wolves were trapped, shot from planes and snowmobiles, dug from their dens, and hunted with dogs. Animal carcasses salted with strychnine were left out for wolves to eat. Unfortunately, this practice also indiscriminately killed eagles, ravens, foxes, bears and other animals that fed on the poisoned carrion.

Constantly persecuted and targeted by large scale predator eradication programs sponsored by the federal government, wolves have been pursued with

more passion and determination than any other animal in the history of the United States. By the time wolves were finally protected by the Endangered Species Act of 1973, they had been exterminated from the lower forty-eight states, except for a few hundred that inhabited extreme northeastern Minnesota. Wolf populations were the lowest in North America in the 1950s.

Worldwide, gray wolf populations are increasing due to research, government protection, and public education efforts.

Have wolves ever attacked people?

SOME PEOPLE CONTINUE to have the unfounded fear that wolves attack people or threaten human activities. In fact, wolves generally avoid people. While wolves have the ability to harm humans, there has never been a verified report of a healthy wild wolf deliberately attacking or seriously injuring a human in North America. Wolves can be very tolerant of human activity if they are not deliberately persecuted.

"We have doomed the Wolf not for what it is, but for what we have deliberately and mistakenly perceived it to be... the mythologized epitome of a savage, ruthless killer... which is, in reality, no more than a reflexed image of ourselves."

—Farley Mowat

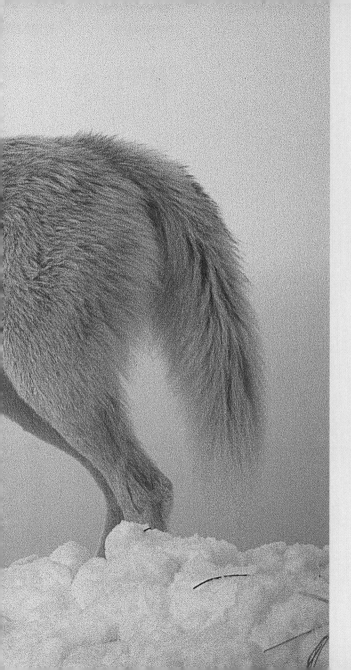

Is the gray wolf an endangered species?

IN 1967 THE GRAY WOLF was federally listed as endangered in a few states, and in 1973 the gray wolf came under the protection of the Endangered Species Act. Wolf recovery under the Endangered Species Act has been very successful, and in 2003, the gray wolf was downlisted from endangered to threatened in the lower forty-eight states.

Endangered means a species is considered in danger of extinction throughout all or a significant portion of its range, and *threatened* means a species may become endangered. In Alaska, wolf populations are

significant enough where the animals are not considered endangered or threatened.

The gray wolves in Canada are managed by provincial governments and are not currently threatened, but in western Eurasia, gray wolf populations have been reduced to isolated remnants in Poland, Scandinavia, Russia, Portugal, Spain, and Italy. Wolves were exterminated from the British Isles in the eighteenth century, and nearly disappeared from Japan and Greenland in the twentieth century. Greenland's wolf populations seem to have made a full recovery today.

Wolf recovery and management are very polarized, contro-

versial, and emotional issues for many people, and often stem from people's attitudes, fears, and misunderstandings more than wolves themselves. Attitudes are often based on inaccurate information, making wolf management perhaps more difficult than any other wildlife management program.

"The wolf is neither man's competitor nor his enemy. He is a fellow creature with whom the earth must be shared."

—L. David Mech

"*I've always said that the best wolf habitat resides in the human heart. You have to leave a little space for them to live.*"

—Ed Bangs

CD Track Contents

Track 1: Timber wolf solo howls

Narration: The vocal repertoire of the wolf consists of sounds that often grade into one another. These include whines, growls, woofs, barks, and howls. The vocalization most commonly associated with the wolf is its howl. This long, mournful sound can often be heard over several miles. With its nose pointed toward the sky, and its lips drawn forward, the wolf howls to notify other groups of its presence and territory ownership, or to assemble members of its own pack. A howling bout may be produced by one or many animals belonging to a pack. Lone, transient wolves with no pack affiliation tend not to howl, perhaps in an attempt to remain undetected by any resident pack with which conflict could arise. Following are howls of a single timber wolf.

Track 2: Timber wolf pairs howl

Narration: Here is a howling bout produced by a pair of timber wolves. At the beginning, you can hear the female whining.

Track 3: Timber wolf howl chorus

Narration: The following is a howling chorus from a pack of timber wolves.

Track 4: Mexican wolf howl chorus

Narration: Next, you will hear a howling chorus from a group of three or four Mexican wolves. The Mexican wolf, like the timber wolf, is a subspecies of gray wolf. The vocalizations of these two subspecies sound very similar.

Track 5: Mexican wolf whines

Narration: The whine, or wimper, is considered to be a signal of submission or friendly greeting. In addition, whines are often heard before, during, or after howling choruses, perhaps as a subordinate animal reaffirms its position in the pack. The following is a series of whines from Mexican wolves.

Track 6: Mexican wolf growl

Narration: Growls can be heard during close physical interactions between individual wolves. These threatening sounds are signals of aggression, and often evoke whines of submission from less dominant animals. Here is an example of such an interaction between members of a Mexican wolf pack.

Track 7: Wolf bark & woof mix

Narration: The wolf's bark is similar to the bark of a domestic dog. However, wolves bark rarely compared to the incessant barking of their domesticated descendants. The barks and lower amplitude woofs of the wolf are usually alarm signals. In the following sequence, you will hear one bark and two woofs from a Mexican wolf, and then a mix of barking and whining produced by timber wolves.

Track 8: Coyote yip-howl chorus

Narration: Coyotes produce the same types of vocalizations as the wolf, and typically in the same contexts. However, the chorus howl of the coyote, which often starts with the howling of one individual, quickly evolves into a cacophony of sound, including barks, yips, and various types of howls. Here is an example, produced by a pack of five coyotes.

Tracks 9-16: All tracks are repeated without narration.